STAND UP TO OCD!

of related interest

OCD – Tools to Help You Fight Back!
A CBT Workbook for Young People
Cynthia Turner, Georgina Krebs and Chloë Volz
Illustrated by Lisa Jo Robinson
ISBN 978 1 84905 402 7
eISBN 978 0 85700 770 4

Can I tell you about OCD?
A guide for friends, family and professionals
Amita Jassi
Illustrated by Sarah Hull
ISBN 978 1 84905 381 5
eISBN 978 0 85700 736 0

Breaking Free from OCD
A CBT Guide for Young People and Their Families
Jo Derisley, Isobel Heyman, Sarah Robinson and Cynthia Turner
ISBN 978 1 84310 574 9
eISBN 978 1 84642 799 2

Touch and Go Joe
An Adolescent's Experience of OCD
Joe Wells
ISBN 978 1 84310 391 2
eISBN 978 1 84642 489 2

STAND UP ᵀᴼ OCD!

A CBT Self–Help Guide and Workbook for Teens

Kelly Wood and Douglas Fletcher

Jessica Kingsley *Publishers*
London and Philadelphia

First published in 2019
by Jessica Kingsley Publishers
73 Collier Street
London N1 9BE, UK
and
400 Market Street, Suite 400
Philadelphia, PA 19106, USA

www.jkp.com

Library of Congress Cataloging in Publication Data
Names: Wood, Kelly, author.
Title: Stand up to OCD! : a CBT self-help guide and workbook for teens /
    Kelly Wood and Douglas Fletcher.
Description: London : Philadelphia : Jessica Kingsley Publishers, 2019.
Identifiers: LCCN 2018028681 | ISBN 9781785928352
Subjects: LCSH: Obsessive-compulsive disorder in adolescence--Treatment. |
    Cognitive therapy.
Classification: LCC RJ506.O25 W66 2019 | DDC 616.85/22700835-
-dc23 LC record available at https://lccn.loc.gov/2018028681

British Library Cataloguing in Publication Data
A CIP catalogue record for this book is available from the British Library

ISBN 978 1 78592 835 2
eISBN 978 1 78450 973 6

Printed and bound in China

Contents

How to Use This Book

Obsessive Compulsive Disorder (OCD) is a problem that affects a lot of people. Fortunately, we now know a lot about OCD and how to treat it. A treatment called Cognitive Behaviour Therapy (CBT) has been found to help many people struggling with OCD. The aim of this book is to help you to learn about OCD and how CBT can help you.

The book is divided into two parts:

Part 1: In Part 1 we will meet three young people struggling with OCD and follow their journey through group therapy. As we follow their stories, we will learn all about where OCD comes from and the ways it causes problems in people's lives. Together, we will discover the steps involved in CBT and see how the people in the group manage to overcome obstacles so that they can get their lives back.

Part 2: This section is a workbook that will help you to use CBT ideas in your own life. It's called a workbook because... well, because to get your life back from OCD you're going to need to put in some hard work! Don't worry though, you will be given lots of guidance and tips to help you on your way.

Although the characters in this book have group therapy, the same CBT techniques are used in individual therapy or in self-help books such as this one. Using self-help is a great way to become your own therapist.

So, let's get started on learning about OCD. We have a lot of work to do...

PART I

LEARNING ABOUT OCD

Chapter 1

So What's This All About?

Today I am going to introduce you to someone who likes to cause trouble, disturbance and mischief. This 'someone' has been around for a long time and affects the lives of many people. He is known all around the world – in towns and cities, in villages and valleys. In different countries, he goes by different names. In France, they call him 'Trouble Obsessionel Compulsif' and in Italy, they call him 'Disturbo Ossessivo-Compulsivo'. In English-speaking countries he is known as 'Obsessive Compulsive Disorder', or as OCD for short.

My name is Dr Kelly Wood and I am a psychologist. I have met a lot of young people who have been bothered by OCD. However, with hard work and determination, these young people have taken their lives back from OCD.

The ideas in this book have been developed by many different people who have met OCD and worked really hard to figure out his tricks and tactics.

Researchers and therapists have spent a great deal of time studying OCD and have developed a type of therapy called Cognitive Behaviour Therapy (CBT for short).

The word 'cognitive' is just another word for 'thinking'. CBT looks at the relationships between your thoughts, feelings and behaviour.

CBT has been shown to help young children, teenagers and adults. These ideas might seem strange and they involve hard work but if you practise them they work very well.

Throughout this book, you will notice that sometimes OCD looks quite small and harmless. You might think he looks innocent or maybe even cute.

At other times you will see OCD grow in size. He stops looking harmless and becomes threatening and scary.

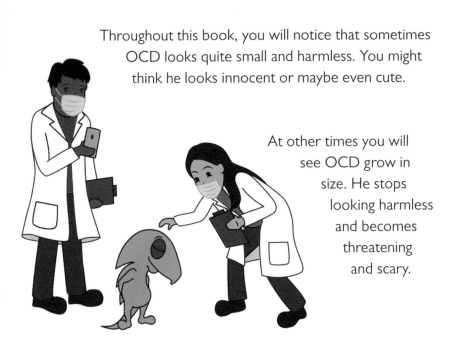

These are both tricks that OCD uses to get you to do what he wants.

Sometimes OCD tries to scare you into doing things. At other times he will try to persuade you to do what he says by pretending that he is protecting you.

You might be reading this book because you have met OCD already and you know about the mischief that he can cause. Maybe someone you know thinks that they have spotted OCD causing problems in your life. Either way, this book will help you to learn more about who OCD is, how he gets his power and what can be done to stand up to him and take that power away.

This book will help you to learn more about CBT and how it helps you to overcome OCD. We will meet three young people whose lives have been affected by OCD.

I DON'T LIKE THE LOOK OF ALL THIS...

Learning about their stories will help you to learn more about the different ways in which OCD can bother people, but also the ways that CBT can help you to stand up to OCD.

In the last chapter of the book, we focus on the things that you can do to get your life back from OCD.

If you are sure that you want to read on – great! If you're not sure, well, why not just give the book a try? What have you got to lose?

Chapter 2

Meeting OCD

Now we're going to meet three teenagers and find out about how OCD sneaked into their lives. You will see that OCD uses tricks to get people to trust him and how over time this helps him to grow stronger.

This is David.

One day, David was getting ready for school when he began thinking about his best friend, Sam. Sam had been off sick the day before and David found himself thinking that he didn't want to get ill as he had an important football match coming up that he definitely couldn't miss.

David used the toilet before he left the house for school. After he had washed his hands he found himself thinking that perhaps his hands weren't clean enough and that he might still have some harmful germs on them.

He decided to wash his hands again.

ARE YOU SURE THAT YOUR HANDS ARE CLEAN? IF THERE ARE GERMS ON YOUR HANDS YOU WILL GET ILL AND MISS THE MATCH.

Now let me introduce you to Sarah.

One morning, Sarah and her mother had a big argument about Sarah coming home late the night before. That day when she got home from school, her grandmother told Sarah that her mother was in the hospital. Sarah was shocked to find out that her mother had fallen down the stairs and broken her leg. When she saw her mother in the hospital, Sarah became very upset. She started to wonder if she was to blame for the accident…

21

Finally, let's meet Riya.

Yesterday, Riya found out that her friend Angela's house had been robbed. She thought about how awful it would be for that to happen. Later that night, Riya found herself worrying about her house being broken into. She went downstairs to check that her parents had remembered to lock the back door...

Riya found that the door was locked and she felt better. However, as she was about to climb back up the stairs, Riya started to doubt that she had checked properly and went back down to check again.

Often, OCD will creep into a person's life when they are worried about something. He will make the worry bigger and bigger in order to get the person to start to listen to his suggestions.

Do you see how OCD sneaked into the lives of David, Sarah and Riya? Over the next few weeks, OCD started to grow in size and become more powerful and troublesome.

Chapter 3

Then OCD Started to Change the Rules...

David started to worry a lot about germs and whether the things he touched might be dirty. OCD began to tell him that more and more things were dirty and should be avoided.

Whilst David was worried about becoming ill, he did not get sick. He thought that the reason for this must be that OCD's strategies to avoid germs were working.

Next, OCD told David that in order to be safe he needed to wash his hands for 10 minutes at a time. David felt that this was worth it to be totally sure that he wouldn't get sick and that 10 minutes really wasn't that much time anyway.

Then OCD started to change the rules…

At first, David's family became angry with him for spending so long in the bathroom. Then, they started to get worried as they saw how red his hands were from washing them again and again in very hot water.

...RULE 23: YOU MUST NOT TOUCH ANY ORNAMENTS. RULE 24: YOU MUST WEAR GLOVES TO TAKE YOUR SHOES OFF. RULE 25...

So what about Sarah? Sarah felt terribly guilty about her mum's broken leg. Everyone in the family called it an accident but she was sure that it was her fault.

Sarah was petrified that if she thought bad things they would come true and this would hurt more people around her. OCD told her that she must not think bad things and that she should cancel out any 'bad thoughts' by saying a vow to protect her family. If she got the vow wrong she would have to start again.

Sarah thought it was worth the effort to protect her family.

Then OCD started to change the rules…

OCD told Sarah that now she needed to repeat the vow perfectly three times. Sarah became more and more anxious that something bad was going to happen to her family. Her parents started to notice that often she was not listening when they talked to her. She would frequently tell them that she was sorry, but when they asked what she was sorry for she became upset and refused to talk about it.

Sarah felt guilty about thinking bad things and embarrassed about the vows she had to recite. At school, she found it hard to concentrate and her grades started to slip.

And how about Riya? Riya got into a routine of checking the back door before she went to bed at night. Then she would check the front door. Then all of the windows downstairs. Then all of the windows upstairs. She would test each lock three times as OCD told her that three was the magic number! Often, she couldn't remember if she had checked the right number of times so she would have to start the check again. After doing this, she felt it was okay to go to bed.

Riya knew that she was being a good daughter by protecting her family. But, guess what? Then OCD started to change the rules...

OCD told Riya that now she had to spend 10 minutes checking that the gas was turned off before she was allowed to sit down to eat with her family. Riya's checking started to cause arguments between her and her family. She found herself getting upset about things like her little sister opening a window when it was warm.

Riya found that OCD was constantly nagging at her and telling her what to do.

THAT LAZY SISTER OF YOURS HAS PROBABLY LEFT THE WINDOW OPEN **AGAIN!** THIS IS NOT GOOD ENOUGH. GO BACK **NOW** AND CHECK!

Can you see how OCD started to take up more and more time in the lives of David, Sarah and Riya? As OCD grew bigger and stronger, they felt weaker and more worried. Thankfully, their parents recognised that they were struggling and each of them agreed to come to a CBT group for young people who were having problems with OCD.

In the rest of the book, we will see how David, Sarah and Riya used CBT to stand up to OCD. Remember the same CBT ideas are used in group therapy, individual therapy or self-help. This means that you can learn to use these ideas in your own life.

Chapter 4

Getting Help

The first step for David, Sarah and Riya was to learn about what OCD is and how CBT can help. In this chapter, we will learn about some of the important things you need to know about OCD. We will catch up with David, Sarah and Riya later on and find out how they used this knowledge to help them to stand up to OCD.

OCD might try to trick you into giving up reading this book by telling you that everything is fine and that you don't need help. Watch out for this! As you may have guessed, OCD does not like CBT at all and doesn't want you to know about it. OCD knows that once you have learned about his tricks he will lose his power over you!

OCD is a type of anxiety problem that affects both children and adults. The 'O' in OCD stands for 'Obsessive' and the 'C' stands for 'Compulsive'. Obsessions are unwanted or uninvited thoughts that come into your mind. They might be words you have in your head, pictures that appear in your mind or urges to do something.

When people with OCD notice these thoughts they feel anxious, disgusted or that something is wrong with them. Compulsions are the actions that people with OCD feel they have to perform to get rid of the obsessive thoughts. These actions are also known as 'rituals' because they are usually performed in a particular way.

Here are some of the most common obsessions:

- Fear of being contaminated by germs, dirt or illnesses
- Doubts about harm coming to you or those you love
- Intrusive thoughts or images about sex
- Intrusive thoughts about God and religion
- Worrying about symmetry and things being in order.

Common compulsions include:

- Washing your hands/body and cleaning objects
- Checking taps or lights are turned off
- Saying vows/prayers in a particular way
- Feeling the need to confess
- Repeating actions such as tapping objects
- Counting.

NA
D.O.
Obsession:
Compulsion: Lining
Notes: Michael has been
with symmetry sin
five years o
scar

Symmetry

Praying

P-Z

Sometimes OCD tricks people into believing that they are the only ones who experience uninvited thoughts. OCD might tell you that you must be bad or crazy for having these thoughts.

In fact, most of us have thoughts that we find unpleasant or disgusting. The difference is being able to see these thoughts for what they are – just 'nonsense' thoughts that don't need to be taken seriously.

You might be wondering where OCD comes from. The answer is that, at the moment, we don't know exactly what causes OCD. However, we know that OCD is not a new problem – it has been around for a very long time.

We also know that OCD tends to run in families so there might be someone else in your family who has OCD. People often feel ashamed about having OCD so a relative could have OCD and might not have told you about it.

YOU PROBABLY FORGOT TO LOCK THE PYRAMID. WHAT IF THE SNAKES GET OUT?

OCD likes to take advantage of people when they feel vulnerable, for example after a person has experienced a stressful time or a traumatic event. What we can say for certain is that OCD is not caused by something you or your family did. It is not your fault that OCD has come to bother you. Nobody welcomes OCD into their lives!

39

But how do people know which thoughts are important and which ones are nonsense? Let's imagine that each person's brain has a thought-sorting captain and crew. This team sorts out which thoughts are important and need to be acted on and which ones can be ignored.

For a person struggling with OCD, it's as if OCD has kidnapped the captain and changed the settings in the brain. This means that the brain gets over-sensitive and starts to treat unimportant thoughts as threats. Threats trigger the brain's panic alarm system and cause you to perform actions to try to keep yourself safe from the 'threat'.

OCD also makes it more difficult for you to shut the panic alarm system down. He likes to keep on changing the settings to make the alarm over-sensitive. This is why Sarah, Riya and David found themselves becoming more and more worried. The more worried they became, the more time they spent doing compulsive rituals.

Let's see the thought sorting process in action and what happens when OCD interferes with this process…

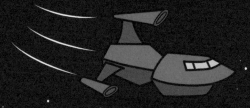

The Thought Sorting Crew in action...

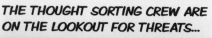

The Thought Sorting Crew are hijacked...

So what can be done to help when OCD hijacks the brain's panic alarm system? Cognitive Behaviour Therapy (CBT) helps you to re-train your brain so that it no longer treats unimportant thoughts as threats. This re-training works in two ways:

- The 'Cognitive' part of the therapy helps you to weaken your beliefs about what your intrusive thoughts actually mean.

- The 'Behavioural' part of the therapy helps you to change your actions so that you can learn to stop performing compulsions.

As you work through the rest of the book, you will find out more about this brain re-training and how it can help you. In the next two chapters, we will learn more about the tricks OCD uses to get you to do what he wants.

Chapter 5

The Compulsion Cycle

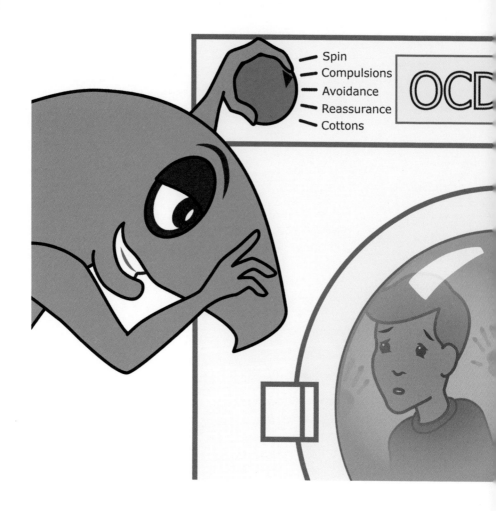

OCD likes to trap you in cycles of behaviour using his tricks. There are three different cycles that he will try to catch you in:

- The Compulsion Cycle
- The Reassurance Cycle
- The Avoidance Cycle.

Looking at each of these behaviour cycles helps us to learn what gives OCD his strength. In this chapter, we are going to learn about the Compulsion Cycle.

You might remember that compulsions are the rituals which OCD tells you that you have to perform. Let's hear from OCD himself how he tricks people into the Compulsion Cycle…

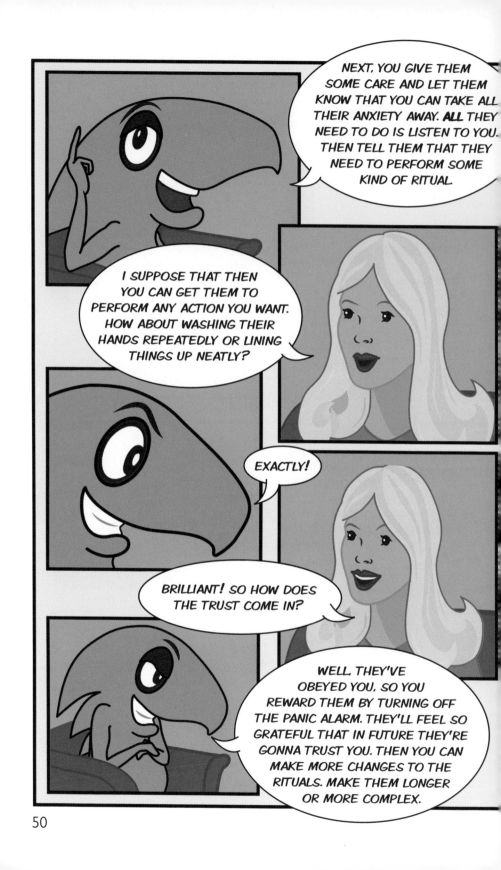

Chapter 6

The Avoidance and Reassurance Cycles

So now we understand the Compulsion Cycle. OCD uses two other cycles: the Avoidance Cycle and the Reassurance Cycle.

These cycles are used by OCD, but they are also seen in other anxiety problems such as panic or phobia.

The Avoidance Cycle

OCD gets you to avoid doing activities that you used to do by tricking you into thinking that they are now dangerous. In the group, we thought about whether there were any activities or places that David, Sarah or Riya were now avoiding because of OCD.

The group noticed how much OCD was causing them to avoid the kinds of things that did not bother their friends or families. They also noticed that these things had not bothered them in the past. However, Sarah wasn't so sure that avoidance was a problem for her…

The Reassurance Cycle

In the Reassurance Cycle, OCD tells you to ask others for reassurance. OCD may tell you to ask for reassurance about your actions, or the actions of other people.

OCD may also get you to seek reassurance by getting you to spend long periods of time trying to find answers about your worries in books or on the internet. This reassurance might make you feel better for a short amount of time, but it doesn't last. OCD always presses the 'Doubt' button which tricks you into asking the same question again or spending more time searching for the 'perfect' answer.

There might be part of you that knows that you don't really need to use compulsions, reassurance or avoidance. However, OCD knows that pressing the panic alarm will make you doubt yourself. It then becomes difficult to change your behaviour because the risk of disobeying OCD feels too high. This stops you from finding out whether the thing you worry about is really likely to happen. As you trust OCD more and more, you start to trust yourself less and less.

We are starting to understand how crafty OCD is. You might not be surprised to hear that OCD has a clever way of protecting himself – he uses your own beliefs to make himself stronger. Let's take a look at these beliefs...

Chapter 7

OCD's Mind Tricks

We have already learned that all people have uninvited thoughts. How is it that OCD has managed to trick you into believing that you should be worried about these thoughts?

Holding certain beliefs makes it easier for OCD to convince you that your uninvited thoughts are harmful. Here are six common beliefs that OCD can use to gain power over you.

#1

YOU MUST ACHIEVE

#2

YOU MUST NOT BE A **THOUGHT CRIMINAL**

#3

YOU MUST BE **THE PROTECTOR**

 #4

ABOUT WHAT HAS AND WILL HAPPEN

#5

YOU MUST MAKE

#6

IS ALWAYS JUST AROUND THE CORNER

OCD wants you to continue believing these things. He knows that people who have these beliefs are the easiest targets for him. They are more vulnerable to his tricks and having these beliefs makes it harder to kick OCD out of your life. It's important that you are able to recognise these beliefs. Let's find out more about them...

This is the belief that if you just try hard enough, it is possible to have complete control of your thoughts.

THOUGHT CRIMINAL

This is the belief that thinking about doing bad things is as wrong as actually doing something bad. If you think bad things then you must be a bad person. Thinking about something automatically makes it more likely to happen.

THE PROTECTOR

This is the belief that it is your job to stop harm coming to other people. This is a full-time, 24 hours a day, 7 days a week, 365 days a year responsibility. If you fail to prevent harm from coming to others it is as bad as harming someone on purpose.

This is the belief that you must be certain about what has happened and what is going to happen. Being uncertain is terrible and you won't be able to cope with it.

NO MISTAKES

This is the belief that you must do things perfectly. Mistakes can have terrible consequences!

CERTAIN DOOM

This is the belief that bad things are definitely going to happen. When bad things do happen, the result will be so terrible that you will not be able to cope.

Imagine that OCD lives in a tall tower made of bricks. The bricks are made from your beliefs. The stronger the beliefs, the stronger the tower. How can we weaken OCD's tower?

1. By using experiments to test out your beliefs. This helps you to find out if OCD is telling you the truth.

2. By practising disobeying OCD and finding out what really happens when you don't listen to him.

First, we will learn about testing your beliefs…

Chapter 8

Testing Out Your Beliefs

In the last chapter, we looked at the different beliefs that OCD uses to trick you. You might have recognised that you have some of these beliefs but you may be thinking 'I'm not being tricked! I believe these things because they are true.' So how do we find out whether your beliefs are true or not? Well, we can test out your beliefs and find out whether OCD is telling you the truth.

Working on 'Mind Control' beliefs

In the group, we discussed whether it is possible to completely control your thoughts. David, Sarah and Riya all believed that this is something that they should be able to do. They believed that not being able to fully control your thoughts is a sign of weakness. To help us think about mind control we did a thinking experiment together…

David, Sarah and Riya noticed that trying not to think about the rabbit didn't work! This experiment helped them to understand that you can't fully control your thoughts.

To find out more about whether mind control is possible I asked the group to do a survey with their friends and family to see if any of their loved ones had partial or complete control of their minds. Let's see what the group learned…

So, the group found that their friends and family also lacked control over their thoughts. They also realised that we would live in a very dull world if complete mind control was possible!

Working on 'Thought Criminal' beliefs

Sarah believed that having bad thoughts meant that bad things would happen. She also thought that she was a bad person for having these thoughts. In the group we helped Sarah test out this idea by asking her to find out:

- If anybody has ever gone to prison just for having bad thoughts?
- If there are any laws against having bad thoughts?
- Whether any of her friends or family ever had bad thoughts?

After researching this, Sarah concluded that if we could be arrested for our thoughts, most people would be in prison!

Can you imagine what that world would be like?

We also helped Sarah to think about the steps that need to happen for a thought to become an action…

EACH DAY FOR A WEEK SARAH THINKS ABOUT KELLY WINNING THE LOTTERY...

SARAH FOCUSES HER THOUGHTS ON PUSHING KELLY OFF HER CHAIR...

Can you see how by collecting evidence, Sarah started to develop doubts about the power of her thoughts? She began to question whether just thinking something can make it happen. She started to consider the possibility that her uninvited thoughts were really nothing more than just horrible thoughts.

Working on 'protector' beliefs

Riya began to recognise that she held strong beliefs about her role as a 'protector'…

Next, I asked Riya to draw a pie chart using this list and divide it up based on how much she believed each item in the list would contribute to her house being burgled. I asked her to add her own responsibility last. Let's take a look at Riya's pie chart...

Looking at responsibility in this way helped Riya to start to weaken her belief that it was completely her responsibility to protect her family from bad things happening.

The group found that exploring and testing out their beliefs had helped in starting to weaken OCD's tower and take some of his power away. Their results are summarised below. In the next section of the book we will discuss the most important way that you can weaken OCD's power over you.

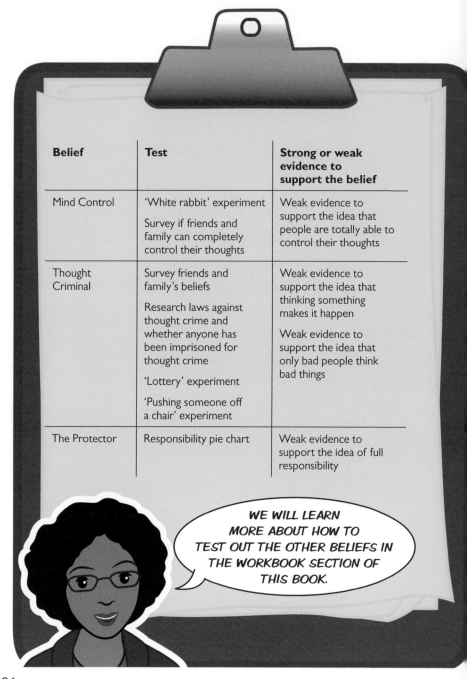

Belief	Test	Strong or weak evidence to support the belief
Mind Control	'White rabbit' experiment Survey if friends and family can completely control their thoughts	Weak evidence to support the idea that people are totally able to control their thoughts
Thought Criminal	Survey friends and family's beliefs Research laws against thought crime and whether anyone has been imprisoned for thought crime 'Lottery' experiment 'Pushing someone off a chair' experiment	Weak evidence to support the idea that thinking something makes it happen Weak evidence to support the idea that only bad people think bad things
The Protector	Responsibility pie chart	Weak evidence to support the idea of full responsibility

WE WILL LEARN MORE ABOUT HOW TO TEST OUT THE OTHER BELIEFS IN THE WORKBOOK SECTION OF THIS BOOK.

Chapter 9

Taking OCD's Power Away

The most important tool that you can use to take OCD's power away is '**Exposure and Response Prevention**'. This is also known as ERP.

'Exposure' means facing up to your fears by exposing yourself to the thoughts or situations that trigger your unwanted thoughts.

'Response Prevention' means that you don't use compulsions or reassurance to try to make the anxiety go away or stop anything bad from happening.

This is how David, Riya and Sarah reacted when I discussed ERP with them.

If this is a new idea to you, you might be thinking, 'Nope, can't do that!' For some people this idea might just sound a bit odd, but for others this idea will be terrifying.

David doubted that it was safe for him to do ERP. He believed that if he disobeyed OCD his anxiety would grow and grow and this would be dangerous…

EVEN THOUGH ANXIETY FEELS HORRIBLE IT'S ACTUALLY A NATURAL RESPONSE EXPERIENCED BY ALL HUMANS. WHEN WE FEEL THREATENED OUR BRAINS TRIGGER THE BODY'S PANIC ALARM.

THIS IS CALLED THE FIGHT OR FLIGHT RESPONSE. OUR BODIES RELEASE A CHEMICAL CALLED ADRENALINE WHICH PREPARES THE BODY TO FIGHT OR TO RUN. ADRENALINE CAUSES MANY OF THE SYMPTOMS WE ASSOCIATE WITH ANXIETY...

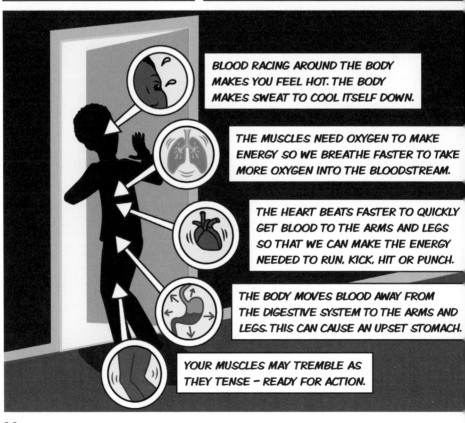

BLOOD RACING AROUND THE BODY MAKES YOU FEEL HOT. THE BODY MAKES SWEAT TO COOL ITSELF DOWN.

THE MUSCLES NEED OXYGEN TO MAKE ENERGY SO WE BREATHE FASTER TO TAKE MORE OXYGEN INTO THE BLOODSTREAM.

THE HEART BEATS FASTER TO QUICKLY GET BLOOD TO THE ARMS AND LEGS SO THAT WE CAN MAKE THE ENERGY NEEDED TO RUN, KICK, HIT OR PUNCH.

THE BODY MOVES BLOOD AWAY FROM THE DIGESTIVE SYSTEM TO THE ARMS AND LEGS. THIS CAN CAUSE AN UPSET STOMACH.

YOUR MUSCLES MAY TREMBLE AS THEY TENSE – READY FOR ACTION.

David learned that OCD makes the body's panic alarm over-sensitive so that the 'fight or flight' response gets triggered in situations that are not really dangerous. When you disobey OCD your anxiety will go up but…afterwards, it comes back down.

Your body is able to return to its normal state without you having to do anything to get rid of the anxiety! We call this **habituation**. This is what happens when you swim in cold water – it only feels cold for a few minutes and then…you habituate. Imagine if each time you went swimming you jumped out because it was too cold? You would never learn that you get used to the water.

Using a compulsion stops you from learning that the thing that you fear does not actually happen and that your anxiety does not just keep on rising and rising.

Understanding how anxiety works helped David realise that OCD was playing tricks on him.

How can we make standing up to OCD easier? The first thing to do is to create an **exposure hierarchy**. An **exposure hierarchy** is like a ladder that you climb step by step. To do this, you need to:

1. Keep a diary over a few days and write down a list of all the things that OCD tells you to do.

2. Think about what would be the opposite of whatever OCD is telling you to do. For example, OCD told Sarah to avoid hospitals, so to stand up to him she visited a hospital. Write a new list with these opposite actions. For each item on the list, rate how anxious you think you would feel about disobeying OCD in this way. This means disobeying without using any strategies to push away the anxiety. Use a 0–10 scale where 10 is the highest your anxiety could be and 0 is the lowest.

3. Sort the list in order from least to most difficult to develop your exposure hierarchy.

Let's take a look at David's exposure hierarchy…

TOUCHING THE TOILET FLUSH HANDLE	10
TOUCHING THE BATHROOM DOOR HANDLE	9
TOUCHING A TABLE AT SCHOOL	8
TOUCHING MY BEDROOM DOOR HANDLE	8
NOT ASKING MY FAMILY IF THEY HAVE WASHED THEIR HANDS	6
TOUCHING THE LIVING ROOM DOOR HANDLE	5

YOU NEED TO STOP THIS NOW OR ELSE THERE WILL BE BIG TROUBLE!

OH PLEASE DON'T DO THAT. YOU WILL GET HURT!

After you have created your exposure hierarchy you need to get started on the ERP exercises. I will briefly summarise the steps involved in doing ERP. We will go through this in more detail in the workbook section of the book.

David, Sarah and Riya began working from the bottom of their exposure hierarchies to build up their confidence before moving on to the more difficult tasks. For each task they:

1. Recorded what the task was and their anxiety level (0–10) at the start of the exercise

2. Recorded their anxiety levels again after 5, 15, 30 minutes and 1 hour

3. Repeated the exercise at least once each day until their anxiety levels were fairly low

4. Moved on to the next exercise on the hierarchy.

Let's look at one of Sarah's ERP records. Notice how her anxiety levels reduced with practice.

Exposure task : Imagine the dog running away

	Start	5 mins	15 mins	30 mins	60 mins
5th March	7	7	5	3	2
6th March	6	5	2	2	2
7th March	4	3	2	2	0

Whilst David was able to plan his exposure hierarchy, he was reluctant to actually start the ERP exercises…

MY MUM SAID I SHOULD JUST ARGUE BACK AGAINST THE THOUGHTS. SHE SAID IF MY OCD IS TELLING ME THAT SOMETHING IS DIRTY I SHOULD JUST SAY TO MYSELF IT'S CLEAN.

HMM, IS THAT SOMETHING YOU'VE TRIED BEFORE?

YES. IT HELPS FOR A SHORT WHILE BUT THEN I START TO DOUBT MYSELF. MAYBE I JUST HAVEN'T FOUND THE RIGHT THING TO SAY TO MYSELF YET.

UNFORTUNATELY, DEBATING DOESN'T WORK WELL WITH OCD. NO MATTER WHAT YOU SAY, OCD WILL EVENTUALLY PRESS THE DOUBT BUTTON. NO ARGUMENT IS GOOD ENOUGH TO MAKE OCD LISTEN FOR VERY LONG.

96

Riya also had some doubts about starting ERP exercises...

Let's see how David, Sarah and Riya got on when they started doing the ERP tasks that they had planned using their exposure hierarchies…

exposure task : Touch living room door without washing my hands

	Start	5 mins	15 mins	30 mins	60 mins
9th March	5	5	4	1	1

Exposure task : Walk into the hospital

	Start	5 mins	15 mins	30 mins	60 mins
19th March	6	6	3	2	2

Exposure task : Go to bed without checking my window

Start   5 mins   15 mins   30 mins   60 mins

19th March   10 - TOO HARD!

Riya decided that she was not going to give up and would find another way to stand up to OCD. She chose to work on leaving the house during the day for 10 minutes without double checking she had locked her bedroom window.

Hearing the rest of the group talk about their experiences helped Riya to feel that she could work on disobeying OCD too. After all, really it was the same problem affecting them all: just OCD in different disguises.

Riya found that after she had done the ERP task, OCD tried to get her to use another compulsion. However, she refused to let him ruin her hard work!

In the group, we learned that OCD will try to stop you from doing the exposure part of the task or try to ruin the response prevention part by telling you to do things such as extra rituals. It's important to be on the lookout for this OCD trick. However, remember that if OCD does succeed you can always take away his power by repeating the ERP task again.

Chapter 10

Where Are
They Now?

David, Sarah and Riya continued to challenge OCD by planning and carrying out ERP exercises and other experiments to test out their beliefs. This helped them to gradually dismantle OCD's tower.

There were times when the group felt like they were making lots of progress. There were other times when they felt like it was all too much and OCD was winning. However, the group helped to support each other. Let's find out more about the progress that they made…

David has been able to stand up to OCD and face lots of challenges. Doing ERP tasks has helped him to learn that he can touch door handles and that he does not have to wash his hands when OCD tells him to.

David started to feel more anxious as his end of year exams drew closer. He started to become more concerned about things being clean. Fortunately, David was prepared for this as we had discussed how OCD uses periods of increased anxiety to try to sneak back into your life.

You might start to feel the need to try and get more control during times when you feel anxious about other things happening in your life. OCD will try to trick you into thinking that using compulsions will give you more control. David was able to recognise that, in reality, OCD had actually made him feel more out of control.

Sarah has been working hard at standing up to OCD using ERP exercises. She has really been pushing herself and has been able to practise thinking about bad things happening to people on purpose.

Although this may sound shocking, Sarah is now becoming more able to recognise that a thought is just a thought. She understands that her thinking is not dangerous to herself or to others.

Sadly, Riya was not able to finish attending the group as her family moved away to another town. OCD thought that this would be a great opportunity to win Riya back! After all, moving house is very stressful. However, Riya knew that she needed to keep on fighting OCD. Riya used a CBT self-help book to continue planning and carrying out her ERP tasks.

Riya is now able to leave the house without checking that she has locked the door. She has stopped checking that she has turned off lights and the gas. She is working on reducing her checking at night time.

At times when Riya feels discouraged, she looks back over the records of her previous ERP exercises. This helps to remind her that she has had success in standing up to OCD and does not have to do what OCD is telling her to do.

KELLY'S CAR IS STILL RUBBISH...

Despite Sarah's thoughts, I still haven't won the lottery and I still have a rubbish car!

Hopefully reading about the experiences of David, Sarah and Riya has helped you to learn more about OCD, and how to take his power away. Now it's your turn to start standing up to OCD. By continuing to read this book you've already made an excellent start. I'm sure there have been many times when OCD has tried to get you to put this book down (or burn it, shred it, throw it in a lake…). Well done for not listening to him. So, enough talking, let's get started…

PART 2

WORKBOOK

Chapter 11

Now It's Your Turn!

Now it's your turn! In this chapter, we will go through the steps involved in doing ERP exercises and belief-testing experiments. These strategies are the key to breaking down OCD's tower and getting your life back.

The ideas discussed in this book will help you to become your own therapist. However, if you need more support from a therapist that's okay. You or your parents can visit your family doctor and ask them to refer you to a therapist who uses CBT. Sometimes people have group CBT to help with OCD but more commonly you will be seen on your own for CBT sessions. You can show your therapist this book and use the chapters in the book to help you plan what you will do to challenge OCD.

Standing up to OCD takes a lot of hard work and it can be difficult to do this alone. It can be hard to put your energy into working on fighting OCD and keeping the problems a secret at the same time. OCD wants you to be too worn out to challenge him so it is important that you ask your family and friends for support. Reading this book can help them to be better able to understand OCD and support you.

LET'S GET STARTED!

IDENTIFY THE WAYS THAT OCD AFFECTS YOUR LIFE

Answering the questions below will help you to identify the ways that OCD is affecting your life. These questions can be tricky to answer so try completing this exercise over a period of one week. It can be useful to ask a friend or family member to help you with these questions.

What compulsions does OCD try to get you to do?

What activities or situations does OCD try to get you to avoid?

In what ways does OCD get you to seek reassurance?
(This can include asking people questions and/or by getting
you to look up information)

What unwanted thoughts (obsessions) does OCD get you
to worry about?

WARNING: You might notice your anxiety level goes up when you
start this exercise. This is because OCD wants to keep control of
you. He will try to make you feel anxious in order to stop you from
making changes. It's important to remember that the anxiety is only
temporary and isn't dangerous.

RECOGNISING THE COMPULSION CYCLE

Next, you need to identify the Compulsion Cycle that OCD is tricking you into. David, Riya and Sarah's compulsion cycles are shown to help you.

DAVID'S COMPULSION CYCLE...

STEP 1
TOUCHING DOOR HANDLES/HANDS FEELING STICKY/ TOUCHING TABLES TRIGGERS THE UNINVITED THOUGHT: 'WHAT IF THERE ARE GERMS ON MY HANDS?'

STEP 2
OCD TELLS DAVID, 'THIS THOUGHT IS IMPORTANT! YOU PROBABLY HAVE DEADLY GERMS ON YOUR HANDS. YOU COULD GET SICK AND DIE!'

STEP 3
OCD PRESSES THE PANIC BUTTON = ANXIETY!!!

STEP 4
OCD TELLS DAVID, 'YOU MUST WASH YOUR HANDS NOW. MAKE SURE THAT THEY ARE COMPLETELY CLEAN.' DAVID OBEYS OCD.

STEP 5
DAVID FEELS BETTER... FOR A SHORT TIME. OCD TELLS HIM TO LOOK OUT FOR SIGNS THAT HIS HANDS ARE NOT CLEAN.

STEP 1
SEEING DOORS/ WINDOWS OPEN AT HOME TRIGGERS THE UNINVITED THOUGHT: 'WHAT IF SOMEONE BREAKS INTO THE HOUSE?'

STEP 2
OCD TELLS RIYA, 'THIS THOUGHT IS IMPORTANT. IT'S YOUR RESPONSIBILITY TO STOP BAD THINGS FROM HAPPENING TO YOUR FAMILY.'

STEP 3
OCD PRESSES THE PANIC BUTTON = ANXIETY!!!

STEP 4
OCD TELLS RIYA, 'CHECK ALL THE WINDOWS AND DOORS. YOU MUST BE COMPLETELY SURE THAT THEY ARE LOCKED.'

STEP 5
RIYA FEELS BETTER... FOR A SHORT TIME. OCD TELLS HER SHE NEEDS TO LOOK OUT FOR UNLOCKED WINDOWS/DOORS.

SARAH'S COMPULSION CYCLE...

STEP 1
WALKING PAST A HOSPITAL/SEEING AN AMBULANCE/INJURED PERSON TRIGGERS THE UNINVITED THOUGHT: 'WHAT IF MY MUM GETS HURT?'

STEP 2
OCD TELLS SARAH, 'THIS THOUGHT IS IMPORTANT. HAVING THIS THOUGHT MEANS IT IS GOING TO HAPPEN. YOU'RE A BAD PERSON FOR THINKING THIS!'

STEP 3
OCD PRESSES THE PANIC BUTTON = ANXIETY!!!

STEP 4
OCD TELLS SARAH, 'YOU MUST USE THE POWER OF YOUR THOUGHTS TO PROTECT YOUR MUM. YOU NEED TO REPEAT THE VOW!' SARAH OBEYS OCD.

STEP 5
SARAH FEELS BETTER... FOR A SHORT TIME. OCD TELLS HER SHE NEEDS TO LOOK OUT FOR SIGNS OF PEOPLE BEING HURT.

Now fill in the steps in your Compulsion Cycle:

Step 1: What is the uninvited/unwanted thought, image or urge you have?
Step 2: What does OCD tell you about this thought, image or urge?
Step 3: OCD presses the panic button = anxiety!!!
Step 4: What action does OCD tell you to do to get rid of the anxious feeling?
Step 5: OCD makes you feel better for a little while but tells you to look out for signs of danger. What signs of danger does he tell you to look out for?

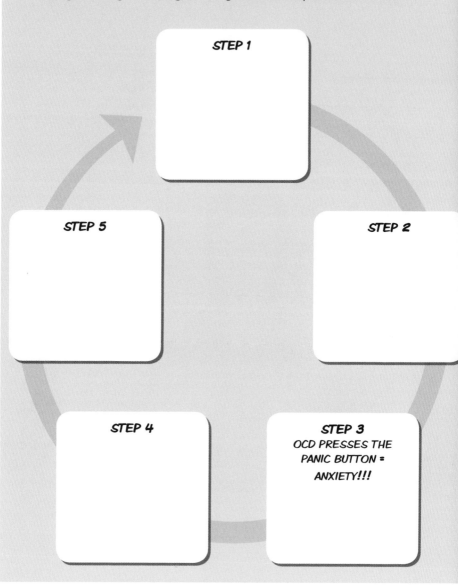

STEP 1

STEP 5

STEP 2

STEP 4

STEP 3
OCD PRESSES THE
PANIC BUTTON =
ANXIETY!!!

BAN REASSURANCE!

OCD often tricks people into the reassurance cycle and it will be important that your family know that you are working on breaking this cycle. This means banning reassurance seeking.

OCD is not going to like that at all and it's likely that he will try to trick you into asking for reassurance. To help with this you can explain to your family or friends that you need them to respond in a different way if you fall into the trap of asking for reassurance.

You may also need the support of your family or friends to stop yourself looking up things that you are worried about. Sometimes it can be difficult to figure out whether you are looking for information that you do need to know or if you are just seeking reassurance.

A good strategy is to build a team to help you with this. Tell your friends and family what you have learned about OCD's tricks. Once other people can spot OCD's traps, they can help you to think through the questions that you are asking. Is this something that you actually need to know or is OCD tricking you into a reassurance cycle?

GET YOUR PEP TALK READY

When facing a new challenge we need to stay motivated to achieve our goals. If you have ever played or watched sports, you may have noticed that coaches usually give players lots of encouragement to help them stay motivated. This is called a 'pep talk'. The steps below will help you to work on your pep talk.

The tasks that you will be working on are going to be a challenge, but you've faced challenges before, haven't you? Think about a time when you had to learn a new skill or a time when you felt anxious about something but faced up to your fear. Write about these experiences below:

These experiences are evidence that you can face challenges. It can be helpful to remind yourself of this evidence because OCD is going to try to make you doubt that you can take your life back.

Think about your goal and why you want to achieve it. This will help you to stay motivated. Answer these questions:

- What will you gain from standing up to OCD?
- What will you be able to do that you find difficult to do now?
- What things will you have more time for?

Another name for pep talk is self-talk. Self-talk tends to be most useful if it's realistic. Saying to yourself, 'I'm wonderful, I'm amazing!' might not be particularly useful in helping you to face challenges. Instead, it's helpful for your self-talk to be hopeful but realistic.

On the next page are some examples of self-talk that David, Sarah and Riya found useful...

Use the space below to write your own pep talk statements to help encourage yourself:

You might want to write these statements down on a card and carry it with you to use when you need some encouragement.

WARNING: Watch out for OCD trying to trick you into turning these statements into rituals. Signs to watch out for are:

- Saying the phrase in exactly the right way
- Saying the statements a set number of times
- Repeating the statement until it 'feels right'.

The aim of the self-talk is to encourage you to face the challenge, NOT to take away your anxiety. When coaches give a pep talk the goal is to get the players ready to face the challenge on the pitch. The job isn't done after they have heard the pep talk – they still have to actually play the match!

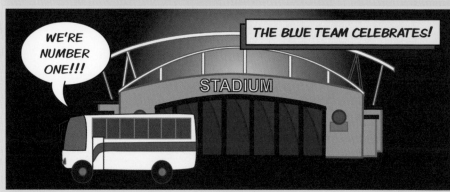

134

IDENTIFY YOUR BELIEFS

Here are OCD's six favourite beliefs. Tick off the beliefs that you recognise yourself as holding. After figuring out which of these beliefs you hold you will be able to plan ways to test out these beliefs and decide whether OCD has been exaggerating/lying or telling you the truth. Maybe you don't fully believe these ideas. You can still tick the belief even if there is only a small part of you that believes it.

*The belief that if you just try hard enough, it is possible to have **complete** control of your thoughts.* ☐

*The belief that **thinking** about doing bad things is as wrong as actually **doing** something bad. If you think bad things then you must be a bad person. In addition, the belief that thinking about something automatically makes it more likely to happen.* ☐

THE PROTECTOR

*The belief that it is **your** job to stop harm coming to other people. This is a full-time, 24 hours a day, 7 days a week, 365 days a year responsibility. If you fail to prevent harm from coming to others it is as bad as harming someone on purpose.* ☐

*The belief that you **must** be certain about what has happened and what is going to happen. Being uncertain is terrible and you won't be able to cope with it.* ☐

NO MISTAKES

The belief that you must do things perfectly. Mistakes can have terrible consequences! ☐

The belief that bad things are definitely going to happen. When bad things do happen, the result will be so terrible that you will not be able to cope. ☐

TESTING OUT YOUR BELIEFS

This step focuses on weakening OCD's tower by testing out your beliefs. You will need to work on testing each belief that you ticked in the previous step.

We will revisit the experiments and surveys that were shown in the group's therapy sessions. There are also some new ideas that you can use. Even though you have already read about these experiments/surveys it is important that **you** try them out yourself. It is really important that you gather your own evidence to find out if OCD is telling you the truth.

MIND CONTROL

'If you just try hard enough, it is possible to have complete control of your thoughts.'

Rate your belief from 0–100: _____%

Try the white rabbit experiment: start by closing your eyes for one minute and purposely thinking about a white rabbit. Now close your eyes again for another minute and this time try your hardest not to think about a white rabbit. What did you notice? Were you able to control this thought?

Write down the results here:

Ask several other people to do the same experiment. Were they able to control their thoughts?

Write down the results here:

Do a survey to see if your friends and family actually have the power to completely control their thoughts. Ask them the following questions:

Do you ever have thoughts or images that 'pop' into your mind? What do you do when this happens?

Write down what you predict your friends and family will say:

Record the results of the survey:

Do the results of your survey support the idea that it is possible to have complete control over your thoughts? Write a sentence about your conclusions:

Look back over the results that you have collected. Re-rate how strong your 'Mind Control' belief is after reviewing the evidence: _____%

THOUGHT CRIMINAL

'Thinking about doing bad things is as wrong as actually doing something bad. If you think bad things then you must be a bad person. Thinking about something automatically makes it more likely to happen.'

Rate your belief from 0–100: _____%

You might have noticed that 'Thought Criminal' beliefs are made up of two parts:

- Believing that thinking a bad thought means that you are a bad person

- Believing that thinking something makes it happen.

We can test out both parts of the belief.

First, let's work on testing out the belief that thinking a bad thought means that you are a bad person. You can follow the same steps Sarah used to find out whether the facts support this belief.

Research the following:

- Has anybody ever gone to prison just for having bad thoughts? Here we are only focusing on thinking about something. This is different to somebody talking about doing something illegal or taking actual steps to plan out the action.

- Are there any laws against having bad thoughts?

THOUGHT CRIMINAL

Write down your results:

Use a survey to further test out this belief. You can do this in person or you can set up an online survey so that your friends and family can give their answers anonymously.

- Have any of your friends or family ever had a bad thought?
- Have any of your friends or family ever been arrested just for having a bad thought?

Write down your results:

THOUGHT CRIMINAL

Next, we can test out the second part of the 'Thought Criminal' belief. This is the idea that thinking something makes it happen. You need to do these experiments without using a mental ritual afterwards to try to cancel out the results. For example, OCD may try to interfere with the experiment by telling you to say a vow to try to keep someone safe.

Each day for a week imagine a friend winning the lottery. Spend at least five minutes twice a day thinking about this.

What do you think will happen?

What actually happened?

See if you can send flowers to someone just by thinking about this.

What do you think will happen?

What actually happened?

THOUGHT CRIMINAL

See if you can cause the roof to fall down on your head by imagining this and telling yourself that you want it to happen.

What do you think will happen?

What actually happened?

Imagine a family member's chair collapsing to see if you can make this happen.

What do you think will happen?

What actually happened?

THOUGHT CRIMINAL

See if you can cause a flood at your school or college just by thinking about it.

What do you think will happen?

What actually happened?

Do the results support the idea that thinking something makes it more likely to happen? Write a sentence about your conclusions:

Look back over the results that you have collected. Re-rate how strong your 'Thought Criminal' belief is after reviewing the evidence: _____%

THE PROTECTOR

'It is your job to stop harm coming to other people. This is a full-time, 24 hours a day, 7 days a week, 365 days a year responsibility. If you fail to prevent harm from coming to others it is as bad as harming someone on purpose.'

Rate your belief from 0–100: _____%

Remember how Riya thought that she would be completely responsible if a burglar broke into the house? This is what OCD wanted her to believe. OCD might be telling you that you would be completely responsible for:

• Something bad that has happened in the past

• Something bad happening in the future.

A responsibility pie chart can help you to find out if OCD might be lying about this.

Write down the event you feel responsible for:

THE
PROTECTOR

Write down how responsible you feel/would feel on a
0–100% scale for this event happening: _____%

Write a list of all possible causes that could contribute to this
event happening/having happened:

THE PROTECTOR

Decide how responsible each cause would be for the event and draw this out on the pie chart (each slice of the pie is 10%). Rate your responsibility last of all.

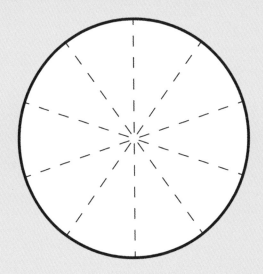

Looking at the pie chart, do you think you are as responsible for the event as you first thought? Write a sentence about your conclusions:

Re-rate how strong your 'Protector' belief is after reviewing the evidence: _____%

'You must be certain about what has happened and what is going to happen. Being uncertain is terrible and you won't be able to cope with it.'

Rate your belief from 0–100: _____%

You can use a survey to see if your friends and family are able to be completely certain about their actions. Ask them the following questions and record their answers on a scale of 0–100%:

1. How certain are you that before you left the house today you cleaned your teeth?

2. How certain are you that before you left the house today you turned the tap off in the bathroom?

3. How certain are you that before you left the house today you flushed the toilet?

4. How certain are you that before you left the house today you turned off any lights you were using?

Write down what you predict your friends and family will say:

Record your results:

Name	Question 1	Question 2	Question 3	Question 4

Do the results of the survey support the idea that it is possible to be completely certain? Write a sentence about your conclusions:

Look back over the results that you have collected. Re-rate how strong your 'You Must Be Sure' belief is after reviewing the evidence: _____%

NO MISTAKES

'You must do things perfectly. Mistakes can have terrible consequences!'

Rate your belief from 0–100: _____%

To test out the idea that things must be done perfectly try looking out for mistakes made by others. Try to notice if your teachers ever make a mistake when they are talking, for example, getting someone's name wrong. Notice whether people on live television such as newsreaders or weather people ever make mistakes when they are speaking.

Over two or three days, write down a list of mistakes you notice and the consequences of the mistakes. Does anything really terrible happen as a result of the mistake?

NO MISTAKES

Now practise making your own mistakes to see what happens. Call a friend by the wrong name. What do you predict will happen?

[ ]

What actually happened? Will this mistake still be important in a week, a month, a year?

[ ]

Make a deliberate spelling mistake on your homework. What do you predict will happen?

[ ]

What happened? Will this mistake still be important in a week, a month, a year?

[ ]

Review your results. Re-rate how strong your 'No Mistakes' belief is after reviewing this evidence: _____ %

'Bad things are definitely going to happen. When bad things do happen, the result will be so terrible that you will not be able to cope.'

Rate your belief from 0–100: _____%

Write down examples of times when you have predicted something bad was going to happen and it didn't actually happen:

Write down examples of times when you have coped with a difficult situation:

Ask your friends and family about their experiences of predicting something bad and finding out that the feared event didn't actually happen. Ask them about their experiences of coping with something difficult.

Record these experiences here:

Based on your own experiences and that of others, what is the evidence that: a) when you predict bad things they definitely happen; b) you cannot cope in these situations? Write a sentence about your conclusions:

Re-rate how strong your 'Certain Doom' belief is: _____%

PLAN YOUR EXPOSURE AND RESPONSE PREVENTION EXERCISES: EXPOSURE HIERARCHY

In this step you will design your own exposure hierarchy. First, let's have a look at the exposure hierarchies completed by Sarah, Riya and David.

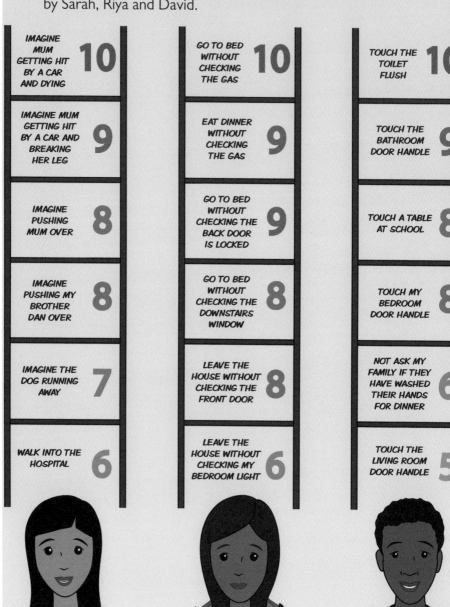

IMAGINE MUM GETTING HIT BY A CAR AND DYING **10**	GO TO BED WITHOUT CHECKING THE GAS **10**	TOUCH THE TOILET FLUSH **10**
IMAGINE MUM GETTING HIT BY A CAR AND BREAKING HER LEG **9**	EAT DINNER WITHOUT CHECKING THE GAS **9**	TOUCH THE BATHROOM DOOR HANDLE **9**
IMAGINE PUSHING MUM OVER **8**	GO TO BED WITHOUT CHECKING THE BACK DOOR IS LOCKED **9**	TOUCH A TABLE AT SCHOOL **8**
IMAGINE PUSHING MY BROTHER DAN OVER **8**	GO TO BED WITHOUT CHECKING THE DOWNSTAIRS WINDOW **8**	TOUCH MY BEDROOM DOOR HANDLE **8**
IMAGINE THE DOG RUNNING AWAY **7**	LEAVE THE HOUSE WITHOUT CHECKING THE FRONT DOOR **8**	NOT ASK MY FAMILY IF THEY HAVE WASHED THEIR HANDS FOR DINNER **6**
WALK INTO THE HOSPITAL **6**	LEAVE THE HOUSE WITHOUT CHECKING MY BEDROOM LIGHT **6**	TOUCH THE LIVING ROOM DOOR HANDLE **5**

154

Now it's your turn! First, list all of the things that OCD tells you to do. For each item rate on a 0–10 scale how anxious you would feel about disobeying OCD without using **any** strategies to push away the anxiety:

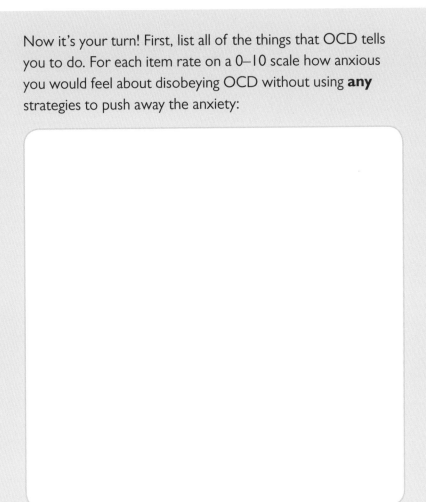

ERP tasks can involve you taking whole steps where you stop yourself from using any of the behaviours that OCD tries to get you to use. However, if taking a full step feels too much, you can break a task down into smaller steps. Remember, there is always more than one way to disobey OCD! You could start by exposing yourself to the thing you fear and then waiting the anxiety out for 5 minutes, 10 minutes or longer before doing the compulsion. You can then gradually increase the length of time you delay doing the compulsion.

Another way to stand up to OCD is to change how you do the compulsion. For example, David worried about touching door handles and felt touching the door with his whole hand was too much for him to do straight away. Instead of starting with this, he worked on gradually touching the handle with one finger without washing his hand afterwards. Next, he touched the handle with two fingers without washing afterwards and so on.

Other ways of changing the compulsion include:

• Doing the ritual a different number of times

• Doing it for a different length of time

• Changing the order of the steps in the rituals.

Whilst it's okay to break the task down into smaller steps, remember that the ERP tasks are meant to be difficult. If a task is easy then it will not help you, as you are not really challenging OCD.

It can be useful to do the exposure and response prevention in your imagination if OCD is getting you to perform lots of compulsions in your mind or telling you to avoid thinking certain things.

Riya often had uninvited thoughts that caused her to worry that she had not locked the door before leaving the house. She would go over this in her mind repeatedly but would often still end up going to check. The mental checks actually made her feel less sure of herself, instead of more certain. To challenge OCD she purposely imagined that she had left the front door open. She allowed herself to experience this anxiety without mentally checking that she had locked the door or going back home to check.

Now you are ready to sort the steps out into a hierarchy. This means the things you fear the least will be at the bottom of the hierarchy and the things you fear the most will be at the top.

Exercise	Anxiety level

As you're reading these steps you might find that you are starting to feel more anxious. Perhaps your anxiety level is already super high! OCD is probably telling you that anxiety is dangerous and that you cannot cope with anxious feelings. He may be telling you that you will go crazy, get ill or even die if you don't get rid of the anxiety.

Remember that whilst anxiety can feel horrible it is a normal and natural feeling. When we face the things that make us anxious we habituate. Our anxiety levels will gradually come down.

TIME TO START DISOBEYING OCD!

1. Start at the bottom of the hierarchy so that you can build your confidence up before moving on to the more difficult tasks.

2. Once you've picked a task, write down what the task is and record your anxiety level (on a 0–10 scale) at the start of the exercise.

3. Start the ERP exercise. Try your hardest to complete the exercise. OCD will try to stop you from doing this and your job is to disobey him.

4. Record your anxiety level again after 5, 15, 30 and 60 minutes. Lots of people fall into the trap of skipping this step but it is really important. Why is it so important? Because recording your anxiety level helps you to gather your own evidence about whether your anxiety continues to increase or whether it decreases over time.

   Use the sheet on the next page to record your results. You can download more copies of this at: www.jkp.com/catalogue/book/9781785928352

5. Make sure you repeat the exercise daily. If that seems like it would take too much time, remind yourself of how much of your time OCD is currently taking up already.

   If you were going to the gym to tone up your muscles you'd have to go regularly and work hard. If you stopped going then what would happen to your muscles? They would start to waste away. Standing up to OCD works in the same way – the harder you work, the faster you'll see results.

What is the exposure task?				

Time and date:				

Anxiety level at start of task (0–10)	Anxiety level after 5 minutes (0–10)	Anxiety level after 15 minutes (0–10)	Anxiety level after 30 minutes (0–10)	Anxiety level after 60 minutes (0–10)

6. You will probably need to repeat each step several times before you are able to move on to the next step. When your anxiety level is fairly low (3 or under) you are ready to move on to the next exercise on the hierarchy. This does not mean you can go back to doing the compulsions you were previously using. Once you have faced a challenge it is really important that you don't reintroduce that ritual into your life or begin avoiding that situation/activity again.

   Let's think back again to the idea of building up muscles at the gym. You might have focused first on building your arm muscles. Once you've built up these muscles you might want to start doing other exercises to build up other parts of your body, such as your leg muscles. However, you would still continue to work on maintaining your arm muscles. Continuing to practise the items at the bottom of the hierarchy helps you to maintain your progress.

7. Continue this until you have completed all the steps on your ladder.

Tips

- Remember that OCD will try to stop you from doing the exposure part of the task. OCD will also try to ruin the response prevention part of the task. He does this by tricking you into doing extra compulsions or seeking reassurance. If OCD manages to trick you in this way, repeat the exposure without using compulsions or reassurance.

- If you find that you feel too anxious when doing an ERP task, it might be the case that this task is too much for you at the moment. If this happens it is okay to break up the task into smaller tasks.

- Make sure you keep the records of your ERP exercises. These records help you to track what actually happens to your anxiety level. This helps you build up evidence that you will be able to use again if OCD tries to trick you in the future.

- Remember it's okay to ask for help. Visit your family doctor to get a referral to a therapist who practises CBT. You can speak to your family or your teachers to help you with this.

Many, many people have found using CBT has helped them to stand up to OCD. Over time you will get stronger and OCD will get weaker. However, it will be important to watch out for OCD trying to win you back. OCD is particularly likely to try this at times when you feel down, stressed or anxious, so you will need to stay on your guard.

OCD can also try to sneak back into your life by making you worry about things that you were not worried about before. Watch out for this – it's just OCD in a new disguise. If this happens, try to remember that the principles of how to disobey OCD remain the same. You will need to revise your exposure hierarchy and carry out new ERP tasks. You may also need to try out some new experiments if OCD starts to use new mind tricks on you.

So, now you know everything you need to know to take OCD's power away! This will be hard work but it will be worth it in order to get your life back.

I hope that you have found this book useful. I wish you all the best on your journey standing up to OCD!